Me Nan, Me Auntie's Cat and the Leprechaun

written by David McNiven
illustrated by Margaret Anne Suggs

CW01664222

To: Grace.

From: Granny and Grandad
12.05.2024

Text © 2016 by David McNiven
Illustrations © 2017 by Margaret Anne Suggs
All rights reserved, including the right of reproduction in whole or in part in any form.

First edition 2017
Second edition 2021

Written, illustrated, designed, produced and printed entirely in Ireland.
Printed by Killarney Printing
ISBN 978-0-9931688-2-6

Other titles by David McNiven and Margaret Anne Suggs
Me Nan Found a Leprechaun
Granny and the Loch Ness Monster

Other titles by David McNiven and Peter McNiven
Granny and the Wild Haggis

Sure, you all knows Auntie Bridie,
She's always out for walks.
She calls in to see Nan, her sister,
An' they
talks and talks and talks . . . .

They used to go out walking,
But sure now, what they really like
Is to ride out into the country
On Nan's new green motorbike.

Mick, Nan's leprechaun, is in da goggles
An' his little face all smiles.
Sure, he's up there on Bridie's shoulder
As they're burning up the miles.

PAT

One evening Bridie says to Nan,
"Wish I'd a leprechaun like that."
But when Mick wished for his brother,
Instead he got a GINGER CAT!

So Bridie put him in a basket,
On a cushion by her bed,
But when she woke up next morning,

Sure, there was a leprechaun instead!

"How d'you do?
Me name is Patrick,
Though me friends
all calls me 'Pat'."

“Ye see sometimes I’m a leprechaun,
But sure, sometimes I’m a cat!”

“It’s something we cannot explain,
Leprechauns can never tell.
Sometimes we’re only leprechauns,
But sometimes we’re CATS AS WELL!”

“Sure, it comes in really handy,
See I loves to climb up trees,
Which is fierce hard for a leprechaun,
But for CATS, sure, it’s a breeze.”

“Sure, now you have your leprechaun,
I’ll make EVERY wish come true!
We’ll have the most amazing fun,
Just Pat the Cat and you!”

Bridie laughed, “Now this is crazy,
I’m sure this can’t be true!
What if I wished for an ELEPHANT?
Would it come here from the zoo?!?”

He shrieked, “You mustn’t say that!”

“Sure, I can’t be stopping the spell!
Bejaysus now here’s YOUR ELEPHANT
And a keeper’s here as well!”

An’ there they were in the garden!
An’ the keeper scratching his head . . .

He yelled: "Hang on for a moment!
This elephant needs to be fed!"

Now Auntie Bridie loved her garden, it was always oh, so neat.

Lovely flowers, vegetables and a greenhouse . . .

. . . a birdbath and garden seat.

The elephant pulled out the carrots,
The cabbages and the peas.
All of the stalks and stemmy bits,
and swallowed them with ease!

Then onto the row of tall green beans,
Sure, she finished ALL the veg.
She ate a few of the flowers,
and pulled out huge lumps of the hedge!

Now, did you ever hear the story?
Sure, I've heard it once or twice.
Some folks do say a huge elephant,
Is absolutely *terrified* of mice!

. . . The elephant found one under a cabbage,

Sure, she made the loudest shriek!
Then she jumped up on the bird bath,
Which began to wobble and creak.

The bird bath was next to the
GREENHOUSE!
They crashed over just like that,
And with a bang,
a crash and a tinkle . . .

. . . the greenhouse was
totally FLAT!

Next the elephant gave a loud trumpet,
And she lifted her little, short tail.
The keeper turned 'round to Aunt Bridie,
You could see his face had gone pale.

He explained, "She's going to do a POO now!
You had better keep well back!
She hasn't pooed since Tuesday . . .
It will fill the biggest sack!"

Sure, she pooed all over the garden seat,
An' the table there as well.
Auntie Bridie stood and held her nose,
It was such a TERRIBLE smell!

The keeper shrugged, “I’m so sorry!
Sure, your garden’s completely destroyed!
I’ll try to get this all sorted out!
Oh, please - Don’t get too annoyed!”

“I don’t know how we got here!
Lord, I wish we were back at the zoo.”
And straight away they both disappeared,
Except for the BIG PILE OF POO!

Auntie Bridie shrieked at her leprechaun,
“I don’t know what to say or think!
Is this some dream or nightmare?
Or have I had too much to drink?”

"I cannot believe what's just happened.
My garden, so lovely and neat;
It looks like the army's gone through it!
An' look at my beautiful SEAT!"

"I'll have to go and lie down now.
Oh dear, Pat, will you give me a hand?"
Says Pat, "I'll fix it this moment!
You'd better just watch where you stand!"

Then Auntie Bridie laughed, says she,
"Pat, I cannot believe my eyes!
Sure, you've made my garden look wonderful!
It surely would win first prize!"

"Oh, I'll have to try my new seat now,
And we'll both have a nice cup of tea."
Then Pat gave his fingers a little flick,
Sure, there was tea and cake for THREE!

"I heard an awful crash," called Nan,
Clicking the garden gate.
"I was sure you'd had an accident -

'Gor isn't your garden lookin' great!"

Gasped Bridie, "You wouldn't believe it!
We had an elephant here from the zoo!
He ate the hedge, the flowers and veg,

Then he did a big pile of *poo!*"

“Look, I’ve got it all here on my mobile phone -
Lots of photos of all the mess.
Sure, now you can see it all for yourself,
Just give this button a press.”

So Bridie gave Nan her mobile phone,
And Nan gave the button a press.
Says she, “Well, there’s your neighbour’s tree.
And there’s the front of your dress!”

“Look, this one’s the clouds up in the sky.
Sure, look now, that’s your shoe.
Now this one- Is it the end of your nose? . . .

. . . Ooooh, but THERE'S the big pile of POO!"

Said Bridie, "My leprechaun fixed
ALL of the mess,
In an instant, just like that.
Well, look now, would you believe it?
He's turned back into a ginger cat!"

So if you have a pussycat,
YOU might get a big SURPRISE!
YOUR cat might be a LEPRECHAUN,
In a pussycat disguise!

the end

A Little Treasure Hunt

How many carrots can you count?
Can you draw an elephant, a mouse, and a leprechaun?
What colour are Auntie Bridie's wellie boots?
How many chickens can you find?
Can you spot two pink butterflies and one yellow butterfly?
What kind of birds are in Auntie Bridie's garden?
What is in Auntie Bridie's garden trug?
What frightened the elephant?
What colour is Nan's motorcycle?
What colour are the zoo keeper's coveralls?
Auntie Bridie grows cabbage in her garden. Do you like cabbage?
What type of cake did Pat get for tea?
Do you prefer cake or cabbage?
What names would you give Auntie Bridie's three chickens?
What colour was Auntie Bridie's garden seat before it was ruined?
If Pat the Cat is 'ginger', what colour IS ginger?
Why does the elephant have a pink bow on its tail?
What colour is Auntie Bridie's dog?
The mouse appears on seven pages. Can you find him?
Can you spot:
a blue snail?
a red birdhouse?
a ladybird?
a watering can?
a green teacup?
Which is your favourite picture and why?
If you met a Leprechaun, what would you wish for?